CARLTON **FOOD** NETWORK

# CHEF ON A S HOESTRING

## Brian Turner

CARLTON **FOOD** NETWORK   From the hit TV series

First published in 1998 by HarperCollins*Publishers*

Text © Brian Turner 1998
Photographs © HarperCollins*Publishers* 1998
CFN logo © Carlton Food Network 1998

Based on the 'Chef on a Shoestring' series
© Carlton Food Network 1997

A catalogue record for this book is available from
the British Library.

ISBN 0 00 414039 7

For HarperCollins*Publishers*
**Commissioning Editor:**
Barbara Dixon
**Editor:** Becky Humphreys
**Proof-readers:**
Fiona Screen, Terry Moore

**Designer:** Clare Baggaley
**Photographer:** Sian Irvine
**Photographer's Assistants:**
Jake Curtis and Sara Epstein
**Food Stylist:** Jane Stevenson
**Stylist's Assistant:** Lizzy Harris
**Photographs of Brian Turner:**
Brian J Ritchie

Colour origination and printing by
The Bath Press

Whether you live to eat or eat to live, the Carlton Food Network has something to tempt your tastebuds. Europe's only dedicated food channel brings the expertise of the world's finest chefs, food experts and celebrities to television screens throughout the country.

Carlton Food Network provides an exciting range of programmes featuring celebrity chefs and personalities such as The Nosh Brothers, Brian Turner, Antony Worrall Thompson, Paul Gayler, Ross Burden, Nanette Newman and many more.

There is something on offer for all food lovers: the great programme line-up features a host of shows presented by the country's top chefs, as well as food from every corner of the world – Africa, India, Italy, China, Scotland, England and Ireland, to mention but a few!

The Carlton Food Network has dedicated itself to ensuring that you know all there is to know about healthy eating and nutrition – so you can really enjoy what you eat. Kids can also try out their culinary skills as the Carlton Food Network features some tasty recipes in a great children's programme – and you can find out how to grow the freshest ingredients to use in the kitchen with the Carlton Food Network's very own gardening slot!

In short, the Carlton Food Network has an exiting mix of ingredients which will appeal to all tastebuds!

Tune into Carlton Food Network, TV's tastiest channel for recipes to make your mouth water.

# The author

Brian Turner gained his experience at some of London's most prestigious restaurants, as well as the famous Beau Rivage Palace in Lausanne. Now chef-proprietor of the award-winning Turner's Restaurant in Knightsbridge, London, he is also executive chairman of the Académie Culinaire de France (UK).

Brian also finds time to appear regularly on television. He will be familiar from 'This Morning' and 'Ready Steady Cook' in addition to his series 'Chef on a Shoestring' for Carlton Food Network. Brian's books include *Get Cooking! with This Morning*, *Ready Steady Cook*, and *Sunday Best*.

## Notes on the recipes

• All the menus can be made for under £10, at the time of going to press. I have assumed you will have basic kitchen supplies such as herbs, spices and condiments, so these are not included in the £10 budget.

• The recipes in this book give ingredients in both metric and imperial, and I suggest you stick to just using one set, in any one recipe. Where a quantity is not given, it is because it calls for a standard packet size, available in any supermarket.

• When a recipe calls for salt and pepper, I recommend you use freshly ground rock salt and black peppercorns.

# Contents

# Introduction

When the Carlton Food Network approached me about doing 'Chef on a Shoestring', I was delighted. I think that too many people believe that eating well means spending lots of money. These days cooking with fresh produce does not mean that you are going to spend more than if you buy ready-made or frozen foods. I don't mean that you should spend hours stuck in the kitchen, slaving over a hot stove. Many meals can be made from scratch in the time it takes to heat up a ready-made meal, or grill sausages. They can certainly be made in less time than it takes to order a pizza!

My challenge was to visit groups of people around the country, and to prepare a meal for 4 people – for under £10. I turned up at their homes, armed only with a camera crew, and had no idea about what I would be cooking that day! We started the ball rolling by discussing what they liked to eat, and then came the good part – they had to give me a tenner! Armed with a rough plan of what I would be cooking, and my £10 note, I set off for the nearest supermarket or market stall. I found that by looking at what was on offer, I often slightly changed what I was thinking of making. One day blueberries were a very reasonable price, so I made a Blueberry and Orange Clafoutis (page 86), which might normally be beyond the budget. The point

is however, that many of the ingredients in the recipes can be varied, according to what is in season. I have mentioned this in some of the ingredients, but feel free to make changes wherever you like!

All the ingredients for the menus on the next page were bought for under £10, except for basic condiments and seasonings that I assume most people will have in the kitchen. In many cases, I bought packets of ingredients, and they were not completely used, so you will find you get a bit more for your money! If you choose to swap around courses from the menus, many will still cost under £10.

'Chef on a Shoestring' took me to a varied range of situations. Most meals I prepared were for family groups, but there were some more unusual locations... One episode took me to the canteen of a large supermarket, where I cooked for the entire staff! I have included the recipes in this book, but have reduced the quantities, to serve 4. Likewise when I cooked for a day nursery full of young children and their carers.

The last thing I have to say, is – try to buy the best quality ingredients for your money, and keep thing simple. That way you will have delicious food... on a shoestring.

Brian Turner

# **Menus**

These are the menus I created in the series, and each one can be made for under £10. The only exception is Menu 2, which I made for 60 people in a supermarket canteen. I have included versions here that will serve just 4! I have arranged the recipes in the book according to starters, main courses and puddings and desserts, so you can mix and match, according to your own taste.

## **MENU 1**
Red pepper and basil flan (page 28)
Plum and lemon pudding (page 104)

## **MENU 2**
Spicy lamb (page 60)
Diced chicken in lemon sauce (page 48)
Leek and sour cream flan (page 30)

## **MENU 3**
Green bean salad (page 15)
Leek and mushroom risotto (page 32)
Poached pears with chocolate sauce
   (page 88)

## **MENU 4**
Onion tart (page 19)
Aubergine, mozzarella and tomato bake
   (page 33)

## **MENU 5**
Melon, mint and ginger soup with
   nectarines (page 12)
Fish and fennel pie (page 34)

## **MENU 6**
Italian bean and pasta soup (page 13)
Baked trout with pomegranate and leek
   fritters (page 36, 38)
Raspberry and almond tart (page 94)

## **MENU 7**
Swordfish steaks with mango and tomato
   relish (page 40)
Triple chocolate terrine with raspberry
   coulis (page 98)

## **MENU 8**
Salmon with grain mustard topping and
   potato pancakes (page 42, 43)
Lemon tart (page 90)

## **MENU 9**
Lemon and garlic chilli prawns (page 44)
Chocolate tart (page 96)

## **MENU 10**
Salmon in filo pastry with dill sauce
   (page 46)
Banoffee cheesecake with toffee pecan
   sauce (page 100)

## **MENU 11**
Stuffed chicken breasts with red pesto
   sauce (page 50)
Plum baked Alaska (page 84)

## **MENU 12**
Minty cucumber salad (page 17)
Thai green chicken curry (page 49)

Melon, mint and ginger soup with nectarines
Italian bean and pasta soup
Cream of pea soup
Green bean salad
Citrus salad
Minty cucumber salad
Muffins filled with leek and smoked mackerel
Onion tart
Asparagus and mushroom tartlets
Baked field mushrooms
Smoked haddock and cheese omelette
Moules marinières

# STAR

**TERS**

# Melon, mint and ginger soup with nectarines

## serves 2

### Shopping List

1 ripe Gala melon
1 teaspoon fresh sliced ginger
1 sprig of mint
(stalk removed)
6 tablespoons orange juice
1 ripe nectarine, segmented

This is a wonderful soup. It is so full of healthy things, you feel good just reading this!

**1** Cut the melon in half, remove the seeds and scoop out the flesh.

**2** Liquidise the melon flesh with the ginger and mint (reserving 2 leaves). Add the orange juice, whizz to mix, then leave to chill.

**3** Serve in bowls or scooped out melon shells and lay a few slices of nectarine on top. Garnish with a mint leaf.

# Italian bean and pasta soup

## Shopping List

2 tablespoons olive oil
1 onion, finely chopped
3 to 4 cloves garlic, peeled
    and crushed
500 g/1 lb fresh or tinned
    tomatoes, peeled, seeded
    and chopped
½ teaspoon cinnamon
1 teaspoon tomato purée
1 small tin cannellini beans,
    drained
2 chicken or vegetable stock
    cubes, crumbled into
    600 ml/1 pint boiling water
1 small packet soup pasta
1 teaspoon mixed herbs
salt and freshly ground
    black pepper

This soup is so hearty that it is almost a meal in itself. Serve with plenty of chunky bread for a substantial lunch for 2.

**1** Heat the olive oil and fry the onion and garlic until they begin to soften.

**2** Add the chopped tomatoes, cinnamon, tomato purée and season with salt and pepper. Cook for 2-3 minutes.

**3** Add the beans and stock, and stir well.

**4** Bring the soup to a boil. Add the pasta, season again to taste, and add the mixed herbs. Cook for 10 minutes, until the pasta is tender, and serve.

# Cream of pea soup

## Shopping List

50 g/2 oz butter
4 thick slices of bread,
  cut into croutons
1 kg/2 lb frozen peas
50 g/2 oz flour
600 ml/1 pint chicken stock
1 packet of mint, chopped
pinch of caster sugar
150 ml/¼ pint double cream
salt and freshly ground
  black pepper

You could ring the changes by adding ham at step 2.

**1** Melt half the butter in a pan and fry the croutons. Reserve to one side.

**2** Melt the remaining butter in a large frying pan, and add the peas. Cover, and cook for 5 minutes.

**3** Add the flour, and stir into the peas. Cook for a further 2 minutes, then add the stock and mint. Stir well, and simmer for 10 minutes.

**4** Remove the soup from the heat and pour it into a food processor or blender. Liquidise the soup, then return to the pan to heat through.

**5** Season, and add a pinch of sugar to taste. Remove the soup from the heat, and stir in the cream. Serve sprinkled with the croutons.

# Green bean salad

see opposite page 49

## serves 2

### Shopping List

500 g/1 lb fine french beans,
  trimmed
4 tablespoons olive oil
1 tablespoon white wine
  vinegar
125 g/4 oz Danish blue
  cheese
1 small packet chopped
  walnuts
1 packet salad leaves
salt and freshly ground
  black pepper

Boiling and refreshing green beans not only tenderises them, but also gives them a vivid, fresh, green colour.

1 Boil the beans for 5-7 minutes or until cooked, but still crisp.

2 Refresh in iced water, drain and pat dry using kitchen paper.

3 Mix the oil and vinegar, season, and crumble in the cheese and chopped walnuts to make a dressing.

4 Mix the beans with the dressing.

5 Put the salad leaves in a bowl or on individual plates, and carefully spoon the beans on top and serve.

# Citrus salad

| serves 4 |
|---|

**Shopping List**

2 pink grapefruit
2 large oranges
2 white grapefruit

This is a very simple and
healthy starter.

**1** Cut the peel and pith off the fruit.
This is easiest if you first slice the
top and bottom off each fruit. This makes
the fruit stable, and you can then cut
downwards to cut away any remaining
peel. Try to save any juice.

**2** Slice the fruit between the segments
and carefully remove the fruit
pieces. Be sure not to include any of
the membrane, and to save any juice
that tries to escape.

**3** Arrange all the fruit in a serving dish,
and pour over any juice to serve.

**Opposite** *Lasagne (page 68) and Flambéed Bananas
with Rum (page 102).*
**Overleaf** *Muffins filled with Leek and Smoked
Mackerel (page 18), Beef Paupiettes with Apricots and
Thyme (page 70).*

# Minty cucumber salad

see opposite page 65

serves 4

## Shopping List

2 medium cucumbers, peeled, deseeded and diced
2 oranges, peeled and segmented
1 teaspoon sugar
2 tablespoons olive oil
1 tablespoon red wine vinegar
6 beefsteak tomatoes, peeled and diced
1 packet mint, finely chopped
1 packet parsley, finely chopped
salt and freshly ground black pepper

I made this to go with a Thai Green Chicken Curry (page 49), so I wanted something mild!

**1** Mix the cucumber and orange together, with the sugar.

**2** Make a dressing by whisking together the olive oil and red wine vinegar. Season to taste.

**3** Mix the tomatoes, mint and parsley into the dressing, then mix together with the cucumber and oranges.

**4** Chill in the refrigerator for about 20 minutes, and serve.

# Muffins filled with leek and smoked mackerel

see opposite page 17

## serves 4

### Shopping List

- 4 wholemeal muffins
- 2 tomatoes, sliced
- 25 g/1 oz butter
- 750 g/1½ lb leeks, sliced
- 4 tablespoons crème fraîche
- 1 tablespoon coarse-grain mustard
- 2 smoked mackerel fillets, crumbled
- 25 g/1 oz butter
- 1 teaspoon grated nutmeg
- salt and freshly ground black pepper

Muffins make excellent containers for all kinds of sweet or savoury fillings.

**1** Slice the tops off the muffins, scoop out the centres and place the muffin cases and lids on a baking tray. Place the sliced tomatoes in a separate dish and warm the muffins and tomatoes in an oven.

**2** Meanwhile, melt the butter and gently fry the leeks until soft. Remove from the heat and stir in the crème fraîche and mustard. Season with salt, pepper and nutmeg.

**3** Add the mackerel and stir again, until heated through.

**4** When the muffins are warm and crisp, fill with the leek and mackerel mixture and top with slices of warmed tomato. Replace the lids, and serve.

# Onion tart

## serves 4

### Shopping List

75 g/3 oz butter
1 kg/2 lb onions, chopped
1 eating Bramley apple,
  peeled, cored and chopped
1 tablespoon cider vinegar
1 packet puff pastry
flour, for dusting
2 bunches of parsley
salt and freshly ground
  black pepper

**1** Melt 50 g/2 oz butter in a large frying pan and gently fry the onions and apple for 2-3 minutes, until the onion is soft, but not brown.

**2** Add the cider vinegar, season, and cover and simmer for about 45 minutes, until sticky.

**3** Meanwhile, roll out the pastry on a floured surface to make a large circle, and use to line a medium-size, spring-form flan tin. Dot with the remaining butter and cook in a preheated oven at gas mark 6/ 400°F/200°C for 10 minutes.

**4** Blanch the parsley by plunging first in boiling water and then in cold. Chop, then mix into the onion mixture.

**5** Pour the mixture into the flan case and bake for a further 25-30 minutes, until the top of the tart is set.

# Asparagus and mushroom tartlets

## serves 4

### Shopping List

1 teaspoon vinegar
1 teaspoon water
2 medium egg yolks
175 g/6 oz butter
1 teaspoon cayenne pepper
juice of ¼ lemon
50 g/2 oz shallots,
   finely chopped
125 g/4 oz mushrooms,
   finely chopped
4 pre-cooked puff pastry
   tartlets
12 thin spears of cooked
   asparagus
1 teaspoon chopped parsley
salt and freshly ground
   black pepper
salad leaves, to serve

These are very easy, and hardly require any cooking. I used pre-cooked pastry cases, and just grilled the tops, at the end.

**1** First make a hollandaise sauce. Start by mixing together the vinegar, a little black pepper and the water.

**2** Place the bowl over a *bain-marie*, or in a bowl over a pan of simmering water, then beat in the egg yolks, until thickened.

**3** In a separate bowl, melt half the butter, then add slowly to the egg yolk mixture.

**4** Season the sauce with salt, cayenne pepper and lemon juice. Strain to remove any lumps, and place to one side.

**5** Melt 50 g/2 oz of the butter and fry the shallots for 2-3 minutes.

**6** Add the mushrooms and cook gently until all the liquid has evaporated. Divide the mushrooms between the puff pastry tartlets.

**7** Take the tops off the asparagus and place to one side. Finely dice the stalks, and fry gently in the remaining butter. Season to taste.

**8** Add the asparagus and the parsley to the hollandaise sauce and spoon into the tartlets.

**9** Warm the asparagus tips in an oven with a little butter and water, place on top of the tartlets and place under a hot grill, for 1 minute, until the asparagus is slightly brown.

**10** Serve the tartlets on a selection of salad leaves.

# Baked field mushrooms

| serves 4 |
| :---: |

## Shopping List

1 onion, thinly sliced
125 ml/4 fl oz olive oil
2 courgettes, diced
3 garlic cloves, crushed
8 large field mushrooms,
   peeled and cleaned
butter, for greasing
8 small slices mozzarella
   cheese
2 tablespoons balsamic vinegar
1 tablespoon chopped chives
4 black olives, stoned
   and chopped
1 small gem lettuce, washed
   and separated
salt and freshly ground
   black pepper

I made this for the Steadman family. Their only request was that they couldn't eat fish or seafood, so I made them this, followed by Chicken Sauté (page 52) and Lemon Surprise (page 95).

**1** Sauté the onion in 2 tablespoons of the olive oil until soft and golden. Add the courgettes and garlic and fry gently, until the courgettes start to brown.

**2** Place the mushrooms on a buttered baking sheet, underside up, and spoon the onion mixture into the centre of each mushroom.

**3** Cover each with a small slice of mozzarella and drizzle with a little olive oil. Season with salt and pepper.

**4** Bake in a preheated oven at gas mark 6/400°F/200°C, until the cheese bubbles, and turns golden brown.

**5** Mix the remaining olive oil with the balsamic vinegar, chives and a little salt and pepper. Add the olives and any cooking juices from the mushrooms.

**6** Arrange the lettuce leaves on 4 serving plates and drizzle a little sauce over each one. Place the mushrooms on each plate, drizzle with the remaining sauce, and serve.

# Smoked haddock and cheese omelette

## serves 4

### Shopping List

175 g/6 oz smoked haddock
  fillet, chopped
4 medium eggs
2 tablespoons olive oil
25 g/1 oz butter
150 ml/¼ pint white sauce
  (see page 68)
50 g/2 oz grated cheese
50 g/2 oz breadcrumbs
salt and freshly ground
  black pepper

**1** Steam the chopped haddock and put it to one side, keeping it warm over the cooking liquid.

**2** Beat and season the eggs. Heat the oil in a large omelette pan and add the butter. Add the eggs and cook for 2-3 minutes. The bottom of the omelette should still be a little underdone.

**3** Arrange the haddock on top, and cook for a further 1-2 minutes, to warm the haddock through. Turn the omelette onto a plate so that the haddock is underneath.

**4** Pour any cooking liquid from the pan into the white sauce and warm through. Spoon the sauce on top of the omelette. Sprinkle with the grated cheese and breadcrumbs and grill until the cheese bubbles. Serve immediately, cut into thick slices.

# Moules marinières

| serves 4 |
|----------|

## Shopping List

50 g/2 oz unsalted butter
1 onion, chopped
2.25 litres/4 pints mussels,
   washed and scraped clean
1 glass white wine
2 tablespoons double cream
juice of 1 lemon
4 tablespoons chopped parsley
salt and freshly ground
   black pepper

**1** Melt half the butter in a large frying pan and add the onion. Fry until the onion is soft, but not brown.

**2** Add the mussels to the pan and pour over the white wine.

**3** Put the lid on the pan and cook on a full heat for about 5 minutes, until the mussels have opened. Discard any that do not open.

**4** Remove the mussels from the pan, leaving the cooking juices in the pan.

**5** Add the cream and remaining butter to the cooking juices and stir until the butter has melted. Squeeze in the lemon juice and add most of the parsley.

**6** Return the mussels to the pan and stir well to coat with the sauce.

**7** Serve immediately, sprinkled with the reserved parsley.

## Vegetarian

Red pepper and basil flan
Leek and sour cream flan
Leek and mushroom risotto
Aubergine, mozzarella and tomato bake
Fish and fennel pie

## Poultry

Diced chicken in lemon sauce
Thai green chicken curry
Stuffed chicken breasts with red
   pesto sauce
Chicken sauté
Jambonneau de poulet
Turkey parcels with potato wedges
   and roasted tomatoes
Stuffed turkey legs with lentil sauce

## Fish

Baked trout with pomegranate and leek fritters
Swordfish steaks with mango and tomato relish
Salmon with a grain mustard topping
   and potato pancakes
Lemon and garlic chilli prawns with rice towers
Salmon in filo pastry with dill sauce

# MAIN COU

## Lamb

Grilled lamb cutlets with garlic sauce, game chips and red cabbage
Spicy lamb
Rosemary stuffed shoulder of lamb with fondant potatoes
Fillet of lamb en croute with vegetables

## Beef

Lasagne
Beef paupiettes with apricots and thyme
Hungarian goulash with apple and celeriac rosti

## Pork

Couscous on the waves
Glazed collar of bacon with Guinness and onion marmalade
Sausage and bean pot with parsley dumplings
Pork chump chops with warm mushroom vinaigrette and stir-fried cabbage and apple

# RSES

# Red pepper and basil flan

see opposite page 97

## serves 4

### Shopping List

butter, for greasing
250 g/8 oz shortcrust pastry
3 red peppers
olive oil, to drizzle
4 medium eggs
375 g/12 oz full fat
   garlic and herb soft cheese
1 teaspoon turmeric
1 bunch of basil, chopped
4 tablespoons chopped parsley
salt and freshly ground
   black pepper

I made this for Bishop Coote and his grown-up children. They requested a vegetarian menu.

**1** Grease a medium-size, spring-form flan tin with butter.

**2** Roll out the pastry and lay it over the flan tin. Push the pastry down into the tin, and trim off the excess. Prick the pastry all over with a fork and line the pastry with baking parchment. Fill with baking beans, and bake 'blind' in a preheated oven at gas mark 5/375°F/190°C for about 10 minutes.

**3** Cut the peppers in half, remove the seeds and drizzle them with olive oil. Grill them until their skins turn black. Remove the peppers from the grill and place them in a plastic bag and leave to cool. When cool, remove the skins. (The steam that collects in the bag separates the skin from the flesh, and makes the peppers easy to peel.)

**4** To make the filling, whisk the eggs and beat in the soft cheese. Add the turmeric, chopped basil and parsley, and mix well.

**5** Chop the peppers into small pieces and stir them into the egg mixture. Season with salt and pepper.

**6** Remove the baking beans and baking parchment from the flan tin, and pour in the mixture. Bake for a further 40-50 minutes, until the top of the flan is set. You can test this by gently touching the top of the flan. If it is very wobbly, it needs longer to cook. Serve hot or cold.

# Leek and sour cream flan

## Shopping List

butter, for greasing
500 g/1 lb shortcrust pastry
125 g/4 oz Parmesan, grated
4 medium eggs, beaten
250 g/8 oz butter
750 g/1½ lb leeks, trimmed
1 clove garlic, crushed
1 small carton double cream
1 small carton sour cream
250 g/8 oz Cheddar, grated
salt and freshly ground
  black pepper

This is a very simple dish, with wonderful flavours.
I think leeks are underused, and often badly cooked.

**1** Grease a medium-size, spring-form flan tin with butter.

**2** Roll out the pastry and lay it over the flan tin. Push the pastry down into the tin, and trim off the excess. Prick the pastry all over with a fork and line the pastry with baking parchment. Fill with baking beans, and bake 'blind' in a preheated oven at gas mark 5/375°F/190°C for about 10 minutes.

**3** Remove the parchment and beans from the pastry case. Mix the Parmesan with one egg and brush over the pastry case, and return to the oven for a further 2 minutes.

**4** Melt the butter in a large pan. Add the leeks and garlic and season well. Cover, and cook gently for 10-15 minutes.

**5** Add the remaining eggs, the double cream and sour cream. Pour the mixture into the pastry case and sprinkle with the Cheddar.

**6** Place in the oven for a further 30-40 minutes until the top is set and golden brown.

# Leek and mushroom risotto

see opposite page 49

## serves 4

### Shopping List

600 ml/1 pint vegetable stock
250 g/8 oz unsalted butter
2 onions, chopped
1 clove garlic, crushed
500 g/1 lb button
   mushrooms, sliced
6 medium leeks, sliced
1 packet Arborio rice
125 g/4 oz Parmesan, grated

**1** Heat the vegetable stock in a pan, until it is simmering gently.

**2** Meanwhile, melt the butter in a large frying pan, and fry the onions and garlic until the onion is soft, but not brown.

**3** Add half the mushrooms and mix well. Add the rice and stir until well coated.

**4** Add the heated vegetable stock slowly, a ladleful at a time, stirring occasionally, until it is completely absorbed by the rice and becomes creamy. This can take up to 20 minutes.

**5** In a separate pan, gently fry the rest of the mushrooms, with the leeks, until both are soft, then stir into the rice.

**6** Stir in the grated Parmesan, to serve.

# Aubergine, mozzarella and tomato bake

## serves 4

### Shopping List

3 medium aubergines, sliced
flour, for coating
4 tablespoons sunflower oil
1 clove garlic, crushed
1 small onion, chopped
400 g/13 oz tinned, chopped
   tomatoes, drained
1 tablespoon tomato purée
a few basil leaves, chopped
2 small packets Mozzarella,
   sliced
25 g/1 oz Parmesan, grated
25 g/1 oz fresh white
breadcrumbs
salt and freshly ground
   black pepper

1 Lay the aubergine slices in a colander and sprinkle the layers with salt. Leave for 1 hour to remove any bitterness. Rinse, pat dry with kitchen paper and coat with flour.

2 Heat the oil in a large frying pan, and fry the aubergine and garlic, until the aubergine is golden brown on both sides. Pat with kitchen paper.

3 Fry the onion in the same oil until soft, but not brown.

4 Mix the fried onion with the tomatoes, tomato purée and basil. Season to taste.

5 Layer up the aubergine, Mozarella and tomato sauce in a soufflé dish, starting with a layer of aubergine and finishing with the tomato sauce. Sprinkle with the Parmesan and breadcrumbs.

6 Bake in a preheated oven at gas mark 4/350°F/180°C for 30-40 minutes, until golden brown.

# Fish and fennel pie

## serves 4

### Shopping List

750 g/1½ lb peeled
  potatoes, cut into
  5 mm/¼ in slices
125 g/4 oz butter
½ glass dry white wine
500 ml/18 fl oz fish stock
300 g/10 oz coley, diced
  into 2 cm/1 in cubes
300 g/10 oz cod fillet,
  diced into 2 cm/1 in
  cubes
50 g/2 oz flour, plus
  extra for dusting

1 medium fennel bulb,
  shredded
65 g/2½ oz cooked
  peeled prawns
1 bunch spring onions,
  sliced (reserve a few
  slices to garnish)
100 ml/3½ fl oz double
  cream
salt and freshly ground
  black pepper

**1** Boil the potatoes for 3 minutes.

**2** Melt 50 g/2 oz of the butter in a large saucepan, and when frothing, add the white wine and fish stock. Bring to the boil, then simmer for 2-3 minutes.

**3** Meanwhile, season and dust the coley and cod with the flour. Fry the fish in 25 g/1 oz butter for 1-2 minutes, to seal the fish.

This is a wonderfully versatile pie. Feel free to substitute your favourite firm fish for the cod or coley. Salmon works well in this recipe, and the price is falling all the time.

**4** Remove the fish and gently fry the fennel in the juices for 2-3 minutes, then place the fish and the fennel in a pie dish. Sprinkle with the peeled prawns and the shredded spring onions.

**5** Add the cream to the saucepan and heat through until just bubbling, then pour over the fish, to cover.

**6** Arrange the potatoes over the fish so the slices overlap, and dot with the remaining butter.

**7** Bake in a preheated oven at gas mark 6/ 400°F/200°C for 30 minutes, or until the top is lightly coloured.

**8** When ready, serve the pie sprinkled with the reserved slices of spring onion.

# Baked trout with pomegranate

| serves 2 |

## Shopping List

- **1 large ripe pomegranate**
- **1 tablespoon olive oil**
- **3 small onions, finely chopped**
- **2 cloves garlic, chopped**
- **125 g/4 oz pack walnuts, coarsely chopped**
- **4 tablespoons parsley**
- **¼ teaspoon ground cardamom**
- **2 tablespoons white wine vinegar**
- **50 g/2 oz butter or margarine, melted, plus extra for greasing**
- **2 whole trout, gutted and cleaned**
- **salt and freshly ground black pepper**

Trout is wonderful served just with lemon juice, but this makes a nice change.

**1** Using a sharp knife, remove the top of the pomegranate, and cut the fruit into 6 wedges. Pull apart into separate sections. Scoop the seeds into a small bowl, and set aside.

**2** Heat the olive oil in a large frying pan. Add the onion and garlic and cook until soft, but not brown.

**3** Stir in the walnuts, parsley, cardamom, vinegar and half the melted butter or margarine. Season to taste, and remove from the heat. Stir in ¾ of the pomegranate seeds.

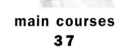

**4** Rinse the trout under cold running water and pat dry with kitchen paper. Score each trout in 2 places on each side, and spoon the onion mixture into the centre of each fish.

**5** Place the trout in a lightly buttered baking dish, drizzle with remaining butter or margarine and bake uncovered, in a preheated oven at gas mark 6/400°F/200°C for 12-15 minutes. Serve the fish sprinkled with the remaining pomegranate seeds. I suggest you serve these with Leek Fritters (overleaf).

# Leek fritters

## Shopping List

2 leeks, split in half
  lengthways and well rinsed
2 medium eggs, beaten
1 small packet fine matzo meal
½ teaspoon dried thyme
½ teaspoon ground cinnamon
vegetable oil, for frying
salt and freshly ground
  black pepper
salad leaves, to serve

I made these to serve with Baked Trout with Pomegranate (see previous page), but you could serve these fritters on their own, as a main course for one person.

**1** Boil the leeks in a large saucepan for 5-7 minutes or until tender. Drain under cold running water. Chop finely, and squeeze in a clean tea towel to remove any excess liquid.

**2** Remove to a large bowl, and stir in the beaten eggs, matzo meal, salt and pepper to taste, thyme and cinnamon until well mixed. The batter should be soft enough to drop (add a little water if the batter is too thick).

**3** In a large, deep frying pan, heat enough oil to cover the fritters. Drop large tablespoons of the mixture into the hot oil and cook until the underside is golden brown, which will take about 2 minutes. Turn, and cook for another minute or two until the other side is brown.

**4** Drain the fritters on kitchen paper and serve on a bed of salad leaves.

# Swordfish steaks with mango and tomato relish

| serves 2 | see opposite page 48 |

## Shopping List

½ teaspoon garlic powder
½ teaspoon Cajun
   seasoning
½ teaspoon thyme
½ teaspoon onion powder
15 g/½ oz lemon grass,
   finely chopped
15 g/½ oz finely chopped
   fresh coriander
1 mango, peeled and dried
2 tomatoes, skinned,
   deseeded and diced
25 g/1 oz finely chopped
   spring onions

pinch of sugar to season
1 tablespoon balsamic
   vinegar
3 tablespoons olive oil
50 g/2 oz flour
2 medium-size swordfish
   steaks
2 tablespoons olive oil
25 g/1 oz butter
salt and freshly ground
   black pepper

I served this with a long and wild grain rice timbale, which is simply rice shaped using a dariole mould.

**1** Grind together 1 teaspoon salt with the garlic powder, Cajun seasoning, thyme, onion powder and ½ teaspoon freshly ground black pepper, to make a seasoning.

**2** To make the relish, mix together the lemon grass, coriander, mango, tomatoes and spring onions, and season with salt, pepper and the pinch of sugar.

**3** In a separate bowl, whisk the balsamic vinegar and 2 tablespoons of the olive oil together. Add this to the tomato mixture, and mix well.

**4** Mix half the seasoning with the flour, then coat the fish with the mixture and shake off the excess.

**5** Heat the remaining oil in a large frying pan, then add the butter. Heat until the butter starts to froth, then place the swordfish steaks into the pan. Sear the steaks for just 1 minute on each side, and then remove from the pan.

**6** Sprinkle the fish with the remaining seasoning and bake in a preheated oven at gas mark 4/350°F/180°C for about 15 minutes, until the swordfish flakes easily.

# Salmon with a grain mustard topping

| serves 2 |
|---|

## Shopping List

25 g/1 oz butter, plus extra
   for greasing
½ onion, finely chopped
1 clove garlic, crushed
1 bay leaf
500 g/1 lb fresh tomatoes,
   peeled, deseeded
   and chopped
25 g/1 oz whipped cream
1 dessertspoon grain mustard
2 x 50 g/2 oz salmon fillet,
   boned and skinned
salt and freshly ground
   black pepper

I served these with Potato Pancakes (opposite), but if you fancied something really healthy, serve this with boiled new potatoes and salad.

**1** Heat half the butter in a large frying pan and gently fry the onion and garlic for 3-4 minutes.

**2** Add the bay leaf and tomatoes and cook for 5-6 minutes, or until the tomatoes break down to a purée. Remove the bay leaf, then whizz in a food processor until smooth.

**3** Place the salmon fillets on a buttered baking sheet. Mix the whipped cream with the mustard and spread over the salmon fillets. Dot the remaining butter over the salmon and bake in a preheated oven at gas mark 5/375°F/190°C for 5 minutes.

**4** Season the tomato sauce, reheat, and serve poured around the salmon.

# Potato pancakes

## serves 2

### Shopping List

250 g/8 oz potatoes
75 g/3 oz flour
2 medium eggs
300 ml/½ pint single cream
1 teaspoon mixed herbs
4 tablespoons oil

Adults and children love these, and they are substantial enough to serve as a light lunch, for one person, with salad.

**1** Boil the potatoes for 8-10 minutes and mash them using a fork or potato masher. Don't make them too smooth.

**2** Add the flour, eggs, single cream and the mixed herbs, and mix well.

**3** Heat the oil in a large frying pan, then, using a tablespoon, place large dollops of the potato mixture into the frying pan. Fry gently on each side for 2-3 minutes, until golden brown.

# Lemon and garlic chilli prawns with rice towers

## Shopping List

250 g/8 oz long grain rice
2 tablespoons turmeric
50 g/2 oz butter, plus extra
    for greasing
375 g/12 oz tiger prawns
1 garlic clove, crushed
1 bunch spring onions, chopped
5 cm/2 in piece root
    ginger, sliced
2 red chillies, deseeded
    and sliced
juice of 1 lemon
50 g/2 oz molasses sugar
2 tablespoons white wine
    vinegar
3 tablespoons Thai fish sauce
1 small packet coriander,
    chopped

I made this for a lovely family, who only get to eat together when Dad's not off doing his Territorial Army duty. I have suggested tiger prawns for this recipe, but any peeled, large prawns you can buy will be fine. Try to use the molasses sugar though, as it gives more flavour than ordinary refined sugar.

**1** Bring a large pan of salted boiling water to the boil, add the rice and turmeric and simmer for 8-10 minutes, until the rice is cooked. Drain well.

**2** Grease 3 small dariole moulds with butter, fill with rice, and press down with the back of a spoon. Reserve to one side and keep in a warm place.

**3** Meanwhile, melt the butter in a large frying pan. Add the tiger prawns and fry gently for 1 minute.

**4** Add the garlic, spring onions, ginger and chillies to the pan with the lemon, sugar, vinegar, fish sauce and water. Cook for a further 2-3 minutes. Remove from the heat and stir in the coriander.

**5** To serve, invert the rice towers onto three plates and arrange the prawns and sauce around them.

# Salmon in filo pastry with dill sauce

## serves 4

see opposite page 96

### Shopping List

1 tablespoon oil
4 x 75 g/3 oz boned skinned
    salmon fillets
125 g/4 oz cream cheese
juice of ½ lemon
75 g/3 oz chopped dill
4 large sheets filo pastry
50 g/2 oz butter, melted
125 g/4 oz unsalted butter
50 g/2 oz shallots, chopped
50 g/2 oz double cream
1 tablespoon white wine
    vinegar
1 glass white wine
salt and freshly ground
    black pepper

You could make this with puff pastry, but I think this filo pastry crust suits the light texture of the salmon and dill. Serve with seasonal vegetables.

**1** Heat the oil in a large frying pan and fry the underside of the salmon fillets for 1-2 minutes to 'seal'. Remove to a plate and leave to cool.

**2** Mix the cream cheese with the lemon juice and 25 g/1 oz of the dill. Season well.

**3** Lay a sheet of filo pastry on a flat surface and brush with a little melted butter. Fold the sheet in half and place a quarter of the cream cheese mixture in the centre of the pastry. Place 1 salmon fillet on top of the mixture, and fold over the pastry to enclose the salmon. You can cut away any excess pastry if you think there is going to be too much. Place the parcel on a baking sheet and brush with more melted butter. Repeat with remaining 3 salmon steaks.

**4** Bake the parcels in a preheated oven at gas mark 7/425°F/220°C for 15-20 minutes.

**5** Meanwhile, make the sauce. Heat 25 g/1 oz of the unsalted butter in a large saucepan, and fry the shallots for 2-3 minutes, until soft, but not brown. Add the wine, stir well, and reduce the heat.

**6** Add the double cream. Bring to boil and add the white wine vinegar. Cut the remaining unsalted butter into small pieces, and whisk it into the sauce. Season to taste.

**7** Lastly, add the remaining dill. Serve the salmon parcels with the sauce poured over.

# Diced chicken in lemon sauce

## serves 4

### Shopping List

2 red eating apples, sliced
2 green eating apples, sliced
juice and rind of 1 lemon
125 ml/4 fl oz Greek yoghurt
125 ml/4 fl oz  mayonnaise
½ cucumber, peeled
  and diced
handful of seedless
  grapes, halved
4 cooked chicken breasts,
  skinned and the flesh cut
  into bite-sized chunks
1 large handful watercress
2 tablespoons chopped parsley

**1** Dip the apples in the lemon juice, drain, and reserve to one side. This will prevent the apples from discolouring.

**2** Mix the Greek yoghurt and mayonnaise together and whisk in the remaining lemon juice and the lemon rind. Fold in the cucumber and seedless grapes.

**3** Combine the chicken and yoghurt mixture together and pile into a large serving dish.

**4** Arrange the apple slices around the side of the dish, alternating between green and red. Scatter over the watercress and parsley, to serve.

**Opposite** *Swordfish Steaks with Mango and Tomato Relish (page 40), Triple Chocolate Terrine with Raspberry Coulis (page 98).*
**Overleaf** *Green Bean Salad (page 15), Leek and Mushroom Risotto (page 32) and Poached Pears with Chocolate Sauce (page 88).*

# Thai green chicken curry

main courses
49

see opposite page 65

## serves 4

### Shopping List

- **6 green chillies, deseeded and finely chopped**
- **2 red chillies, deseeded and finely chopped**
- **2 limes, both zested and 1 squeezed**
- **1 Thai herb pack (red chillies, coriander and lemon grass), finely chopped**
- **4 skinned chicken breasts, cut into strips**
- **1 tablespoon olive oil**
- **6 shallots, finely chopped**
- **15 cm/6 in piece of root ginger, chopped**
- **2 garlic cloves, finely chopped**
- **1 tablespoon ground cumin**
- **1 tablespoon green peppercorns**
- **small handful of citrus (kaffir) leaves**
- **1 tablespoon Thai fish sauce**
- **400 ml/14 fl oz coconut milk**
- **small handful of chopped coriander, to garnish**

Jasmine rice would be ideal to serve with this dish, and is now widely available.

**1** Mix together the chillies, lime juice and zest, Thai herb pack and a little salt. Pour over the chicken and leave to marinate for 2-3 hours.

**2** Heat the oil in a large frying pan and gently fry the shallots, ginger and garlic, until the shallots are soft, but not brown.

**3** Add the chicken, with the marinade, and cook for about 5 minutes on a medium heat, then add the cumin, peppercorns, citrus leaves and fish sauce and simmer for 2-3 minutes.

**4** Finally, add the coconut milk and simmer for 10-15 minutes.

**5** Serve the curry garnished with the chopped coriander.

# Stuffed chicken breasts with red pesto sauce

serves 4

## Shopping List

4 red peppers, deseeded
  and cut into quarters
olive oil
4 chicken breasts
  (with skin on)
1 small basil plant,
  chopped
1 jar of red pesto sauce

I served this with some char-grilled carrots, courgettes, parsnips and red onion. You can buy them all within the budget!

**1** Place the red peppers on a baking tray and drizzle over some olive oil. Place the peppers under a very hot grill, and grill until their skins turn black. You will need to turn them occasionally.

**2** Remove the peppers from the grill and place in a plastic bag and leave to cool (the condensation that collects in the bag separates the skin from the flesh, making the peppers easy to peel).

**3** Mix together the chopped basil and the red pesto sauce, and season to taste.

**4** Cut a pocket in a chicken breast and place 4 pieces of grilled pepper inside. Spoon a generous amount of the pesto mixture on top of the pepper, and fold over the chicken breast to make a parcel.

**5** Wrap the chicken breast in tin foil to make a neat parcel. Repeat with the remaining 3 chicken breasts. Place the parcels on a baking sheet and roast in a preheated oven at gas mark 5/ 375°F/190°C for about 20 minutes. Check to see if the chicken juices run clear, and serve.

# Chicken sauté

## serves 4

### Shopping List

75 g/3 oz unsalted butter
2 large onions, sliced
2 red peppers, deseeded
   and sliced
1.5 kg/3½ lb chicken joints
250 g/8 oz back bacon,
   cut into large pieces
500 g/1 lb button
   mushrooms
16 cloves garlic
300 ml/½ pint chicken stock
1 glass of red wine
16 new potatoes
1 packet parsley, chopped

**1** Heat the butter in a large frying pan, and fry the onion and pepper until golden brown. Remove to a warm plate.

**2** Put the chicken and bacon into the pan, and cook until brown. Add the button mushrooms, and return the onions and peppers to the pan. Cover with a lid and cook for 5-10 minutes.

**3** Meanwhile, boil the garlic in water for about 10 minutes, and leave to cool.

**4** Add the garlic to the pan with the stock and red wine. Bring to the boil, then add the potatoes. Reduce the heat and simmer for 10 minutes, until the potatoes are cooked.

**5** Transfer to a warm serving dish, and serve sprinkled with the parsley.

# Jambonneau de poulet

## serves 4

### Shopping List

6 large chicken legs, meat
  removed from 2 legs and
  chopped, the 4 remaining
  legs, skinned and boned
1 red pepper, chopped
1 bunch basil, chopped
1 medium egg
4 slices bacon
1 tablespoon olive oil
150 ml/¼ pint chicken stock
1 glass red wine
250 g/8 oz spaghetti
50 g/2 oz butter
2 potatoes, cut into cubes
500 g/1 lb broccoli, cut
  into florets
6 tomatoes, quartered
  and deseeded
salt and freshly ground
  black pepper

**1** Mix the chopped chicken with the red pepper and basil. Season, and add the egg, and use to stuff the 4 chicken legs. Cover each with a slice of bacon. Tie with string to secure.

**2** Heat the oil in a large frying pan, and brown the chicken legs. Place in a dish with the chicken stock and red wine and bake in a preheated oven at gas mark 4/ 350°F/180°C for about 35 minutes.

**3** Meanwhile, boil the spaghetti for 10 minutes. Drain into a serving dish and toss in half the butter. Fry the potatoes in the remaining butter until brown and crispy. Steam the broccoli for 4-5 minutes.

**4** To serve, check everything is piping hot, then arrange the chicken legs on the spaghetti.

**5** Mix the potatoes with the tomatoes, and mix with the chicken. Sprinkle the broccoli over the top to serve.

# Turkey parcels with potato wedges and roasted tomatoes

see opposite page 64

## serves 4

### Shopping List

**FOR THE TURKEY PARCELS**
4 turkey breasts
4 small slices ham
4 medium slices of Gruyère cheese
1 medium egg, beaten
flour, to coat
breadcrumbs, to coat
1 small packet parsley, chopped
1 tablespoon olive oil
50 g/2 oz butter

**FOR THE POTATO WEDGES**
4 large baking potatoes
4 tablespoons oil
2 tablespoons Chinese five-spice

**FOR THE ROASTED TOMATOES**
1 tablespoon olive oil
6 large tomatoes, cut in half
small handful basil, freshly
  chopped
salt and freshly ground
  black pepper

This is my version of Turkey 'Cordon Bleu'. You could also use chicken for this recipe.

**1** Place a turkey breast in a plastic bag and bash with a rolling pin until flat.

**2** Fold a slice of ham, and place it in the centre of the turkey breast. Top with a slice of Gruyère, and fold over the edges to make a parcel.

**3** Pour the beaten egg onto one plate, and the flour onto another. Mix the breadcrumbs and parsley (reserve 1 tablespoon of parsley), and place on a third plate. Pat the breast into a shape, making sure it is sealed at the edges. Repeat with the remaining 3 turkey breasts.

**4** Dip each turkey parcel first in the flour, then the beaten egg, and finally in the breadcrumb mix until fully coated.

**5** Heat the oil in a large frying pan and gently fry the turkey parcels for 15 minutes. Turn them over halfway through the cooking time.

**6** Melt the butter in a separate pan and add the reserved parsley. Heat through for 1-2 minutes.

**7** Place the turkey parcels in a serving dish and pour over the butter and parsley sauce, and serve with the Potato Wedges and Roasted Tomatoes.

# Potato wedges

**1** Boil the potatoes whole for 12-15 minutes, then cut them into thick wedges, about 2.5 cm/ 1 in thick.

**2** Place the wedges in a baking tray, season well, and drizzle half the oil over them.

**3** Mix the remaining oil with the Chinese five-spice and pour over the potatoes.

**4** Bake in a preheated oven at gas mark 5/ 375°F/190°C for 10-15 minutes, until the potatoes are cooked through.

# Roasted tomatoes

**1** Pour the olive oil over the tomatoes and season.

**2** Scatter the chopped fresh basil over the tomatoes, and bake in a preheated oven at gas mark 5/ 375°F/190°C for 15-20 minutes.

# Stuffed turkey legs with lentil sauce

serves 4

## Shopping List

- 75 g/3 oz butter
- 4 spring onions, chopped
- 250 g/8 oz dried red lentils
- 150 ml/¼ pint water
- 600 ml/1 pint chicken stock
- 250 g/8 oz button mushrooms, trimmed and cut in half
- 125 g/4 oz white breadcrumbs
- 1 medium egg, beaten
- 2 large turkey legs, thigh bone removed
- 1 tablespoon olive oil
- 2 tablespoons chopped parsley
- 1 glass white wine
- 2 tablespoons chopped rosemary

Serve this with Potato Wedges (page 55) and a selection of steamed or boiled vegetables.

**1** To make the lentil sauce, melt 25 g/ 1 oz of the butter in a large frying pan. Add the chopped spring onions and lentils and fry gently, until the onion is soft, but not brown.

**2** Season well, and add the water and half the chicken stock. Bring to the boil, and then simmer for 15 minutes.

**3** Meanwhile, in a separate pan, melt 25 g/1 oz butter. Add half the mushrooms and cook for 4-5 minutes, until they start to soften. Add the breadcrumbs and egg, and stir well to mix.

**4** Season the inside of each turkey leg and stuff with the breadcrumb and mushroom mixture. Tie each leg tightly with string.

**5** Heat the oil in a large frying pan and brown the turkey legs in the pan on the open side only, to seal in the stuffing.

**6** Place the turkey legs in a large roasting tray and bake in a preheated oven at gas mark 5/ 190°C/375°F for 15 minutes.

**7** Meanwhile, melt the remaining butter, and fry the remaining mushrooms, for 4-5 minutes, until they start to colour. Add the white wine, rosemary, and the remaining chicken stock, and stir well. Pour over the turkey legs, and cook for a further 20 minutes.

**8** Remove the turkey legs from the roasting tray and serve with the lentil sauce poured over.

# Grilled lamb cutlets with garlic sauce, game chips and red cabbage

## serves 2–3

### Shopping List

**FOR THE GRILLED LAMB CUTLETS**
2 bulbs garlic, split into cloves, but unpeeled
4 tablespoons milk
1 teaspoon sugar
1 tablespoon vegetable oil
250 ml/8 fl oz chicken stock
6 small lamb cutlets
1 teaspoon dried thyme
1 teaspoon dried rosemary
175 ml/6 fl oz double cream

**FOR THE GAME CHIPS**
2 large potatoes, peeled
vegetable oil, for deep frying

**FOR THE RED CABBAGE**
2 tablespoons oil
1 small onion, finely sliced
1 tablespoon sugar
1 large cooking apple, peeled, cored and sliced
1 small red cabbage, finely shredded
1 tablespoon white wine vinegar
1 tablespoon soy sauce
2 bay leaves
5 tablespoons water
salt and freshly ground black pepper

**1** Place the garlic in a small pan and pour over the milk. Bring to the boil, then simmer for 1 minute, drain, and mix the garlic with the sugar and oil.

**2** Roast the coated garlic in a preheated oven at gas mark 4/350°F/180°C for 20 minutes until golden, then leave to cool. Reserve 3 cloves for decoration, and peel the rest. Discard the peel, and chop roughly.

**3** Heat the stock in a small pan, then add the chopped garlic. Simmer for 10 minutes.

**4** Meanwhile, place the cutlets on a preheated grill pan, and sprinkle with the dried thyme and rosemary. Grill for 8-15 minutes, according to taste.

**5** After your sauce has simmered for 10 minutes, remove from the heat and sieve, forcing the soft garlic through. Return to the pan, add the cream and warm through again.

**6** Season the sauce to taste. Serve the cutlets with the sauce poured over, garnished with the reserved garlic cloves and with the game chips and red cabbage.

## Game chips

**1** Use a mandolin to slice the potatoes, or slice them very finely with a very sharp knife.

**2** Dry the potatoes using kitchen paper, then deep fry them in very hot oil for about 10 minutes until golden brown.

## Red Cabbage

**1** Heat the oil in a large frying pan and fry the onion until golden brown.

**2** Add the sugar and the apple and continue cooking until the apple is soft, fluffy and caramel-coloured.

**3** Add the cabbage, vinegar, soy sauce, bay leaves and water. Season, and stir well to coat the cabbage. Cover with a tight-fitting lid and simmer gently for 1 hour. Season to taste again, before serving.

# Spicy lamb

serves 4

## Shopping List

750 g/1½ lb diced lean lamb
1 tablespoon olive oil
1 medium onion,
   chopped
2 cloves garlic, chopped
2 green chillies, deseeded
   and sliced
1 teaspoon allspice
1 tablespoon curry powder
1 tablespoon tomato purée
400 ml/14 fl oz coconut milk
300 ml/½ pint chicken stock
2 carrots, diced
1 small tin pineapple chunks
1 small tub crème fraîche
1 small packet mint, chopped

I served this with plain, boiled rice, with 1 teaspoon of turmeric stirred in, to add colour and extra flavour. This was another of my dishes for the supermarket canteen!

**1** Heat a large, non-stick frying pan and dry-fry the lamb. Make sure you stir it all the time to prevent it from sticking to the pan.

**2** In a separate pan, heat the oil and fry the onion, garlic and chillies, until the onion is soft, but not brown.

**3** Add the allspice and curry powder. Cook for 2-3 minutes to release the flavours of the spices. Pour over the lamb, and stir well.

**4** Add the tomato purée, coconut milk and chicken stock. Bring to the boil, then cover and simmer for about about 10 minutes.

**5** Add the carrots and pineapple and continue to simmer for a further 30 minutes.

**6** Just before serving, gently stir in the crème fraîche and scatter over the chopped mint, to serve.

# Rosemary stuffed shoulder of lamb with grilled vegetables

## serves 4

### Shopping List

250 g/8 oz beef
   sausage meat
125 g/4 oz breadcrumbs
3 sprigs rosemary,
   chopped
1 medium egg
whole shoulder lamb, boned
2 tablespoons olive oil
1 red pepper, quartered
1 yellow pepper, quartered
1 green pepper, quartered
4 courgettes, sliced
4 red onions, sliced into
   rings
1 aubergine, sliced

This was the first meal I made for the 'Chef on a Shoestring' series. I made this for a Jewish family, so I have used beef sausage meat rather than pork. I served this with Fondant Potatoes (overleaf).

**1** Mix the sausage meat, breadcrumbs, rosemary and egg together, and season well.

**2** Stuff the lamb with the mixture and then tie firmly with string, so the lamb keeps its shape during cooking.

**3** Heat half the oil in a large frying pan and fry the joint for 2-3 minutes to 'seal' it.

**4** Roast the lamb in a preheated oven at gas mark 6/400°F/200°C for 1½ hours.

**5** Meanwhile, heat the remaining oil in a large frying pan, and fry the peppers, courgettes, onion and aubergine for 2 minutes. Transfer to a griddle pan and cook, until the vegetables are ready and with attractive griddle marks.

**6** Serve the lamb on a bed of the grilled vegetables with the Fondant Potatoes.

# Fondant potatoes

## serves 4

### Shopping List

4 large baking potatoes,
  peeled and cut into
  barrel shapes, 5 cm/2 in
  in length
300 ml/½ pint chicken
  or vegetable stock
25 g/1 oz unsalted butter
salt and freshly ground
  black pepper
1 packet parsley, chopped

**1** Place the potatoes in a deep roasting tray. Pour over enough stock to cover half way up the potatoes. Dot the butter over the potatoes, and season well.

**2** Place in preheated oven and bake at gas mark 7/425°F/220°C for about 25 minutes, until the potatoes are golden brown and the stock greatly reduced.

**3** Scoop the potatoes out of the cooking liquid, drain, and serve sprinkled with the parsley.

**Opposite** *Turkey Parcels with Potato Wedges and Roasted Tomatoes (page 54, 55), Tarte Tatin (page 92).*
**Overleaf** *Minty Cucumber Salad (page 17), Thai Green Chicken Curry (page 49).*

# Onion and ginger marmalade

| serves 4 |
|---|

## Shopping List

2 tablespoons olive oil
2 large onions, sliced
1 sprig rosemary
1 glass dry white wine
2 tablespoons white wine
  vinegar
5 cm/2 in piece of root ginger
4 tablespoons soft brown sugar

This can be served warm, with a roast, or cold, with cold meats.

**1** Heat the oil in a large frying pan. Add the onion and rosemary, and cook for 3-4 minutes until the onion is softened, but not brown.

**2** Add the white wine and vinegar, and heat until the liquid has disappeared.

**3** Stir in the ginger and sugar, and heat gently until the sugar dissolves, and becomes caramelised.

# Fillet of lamb *en croûte*

## Shopping List

1 packet puff pastry
2 neck fillets of lamb
1 teaspoon olive oil
2 medium eggs, beaten
8 pancakes
   (10 cm/5 in diameter)
300 g/10 oz mushrooms,
   chopped
50 g/2 oz smooth chicken
   liver pâté
salt and freshly ground
   black pepper

This is delicious served with new potatoes and green beans.

**1** Cut the pastry into 4, and roll 1 piece into a square, approximately 15 cm/ 6 in square. In order to fold the pastry neatly around the lamb fillets, you need to make some small cuts. Place a knife at one corner of the square as if you were going to cut diagonally across. Move the knife 2 cm/1 in along the edge of the square and make a 2 cm/1 in cut. Make a similar cut, so the cuts are 2 cm/1 in apart. Repeat this on each corner of the square, then repeat for the remaining 3 pieces of pastry.

**2** Heat the olive oil in a large frying pan, and gently fry the lamb fillets for 1-2 minutes, on both sides, to seal them. Remove from the heat and set aside to cool. Season with salt and pepper.

**3** Meanwhile, brush some beaten egg onto the pastry squares and place two pancakes in the middle of each, side-by-side, but slightly overlapping. Spread 15 g/½ oz pâté in the centre of each square, then spoon the mushrooms over the pâté. Place a fillet of lamb on top.

**4** To fold up the squares, start with a long side, and fold it over the lamb. Brush with some beaten egg, then fold in the 2 ends. Brush with more egg, then fold over the last side. Repeat with the remaining 3 parcels.

**5** Roll over the parcels so the folds are on the bottom and re-shape a little if necessary. Brush all over once more with beaten egg and then prick with a fork to allow the steam to escape, when cooking. Bake in a preheated oven at gas mark 6/400°F/200°C for 20-25 minutes.

# Lasagne

Lasagne is so easy and versatile – try substituting chicken or fish, for the beef.

**serves 4**

see opposite page 16

## Shopping List

**FOR THE LASAGNE**
butter, for greasing
16 sheets lasagne
125 g/4 oz Cheddar,
    grated
25 g/1 oz Parmesan,
    grated

**FOR THE MEAT SAUCE**
4 tablespoons olive oil
1 onion, chopped
1 clove garlic, chopped
500 g/1 lb minced beef
1 sprig fresh thyme
1 bay leaf

4 large, ripe tomatoes,
    skinned, deseeded and
    chopped
1 glass red wine
1.2 litres/2 pints beef
    stock

**FOR THE WHITE SAUCE**
125 g/4 oz butter or
    margarine
125 g/4 oz plain flour
600 ml/1 pint milk
salt and freshly
    ground pepper

**1** To assemble the lasagne, spoon some meat sauce into the bottom of a buttered, medium-size, baking dish, followed by a layer of pasta, then a layer of white sauce. Season with black pepper. Continue to layer with meat sauce, pasta and white sauce until you have used all the ingredients, finishing with a layer of white sauce. Sprinkle the Cheddar and Parmesan over the top.

**2** Bake in a preheated oven at gas mark 6/ 400°F/200°C for 10 minutes then lower to gas mark 4/ 350°F/180°C and continue to cook for 40 minutes. Grill under a hot grill for 2-3 minutes to colour the top, if necessary.

## NOTE

**To make individual lasagnes, cook the lasagne, then cut it into 5 cm/2 in circles with a cutter. Place a piece of pasta in the cutter, followed by the meat sauce, pasta, then white sauce and top with the cheese. Carefully push the lasagnes onto a baking sheet, and repeat.**

## Meat sauce

**1** Heat the oil in a large frying pan, and gently fry the onion and garlic until the onion is soft, but not brown.

**2** Add the mince and cook for about 5 minutes, until lightly brown.

**3** Add the thyme, bay leaf and tomatoes and cook for 20 minutes.

**4** Add the glass of wine and the stock and cook for 10 minutes, until the sauce is thickened.

## White sauce

**1** Melt the butter or margarine in a saucepan and stir in the flour. Cook gently for 1 minute over a low heat, without browning.

**2** Gradually add the milk, stirring continuously with a wire whisk, until the sauce boils and thickens.

**3** Reduce the heat and simmer for 5 minutes. Season with salt and pepper. If wished, you could add grated nutmeg, cheese, parsley or other herbs to flavour the sauce.

# Beef paupiettes with apricots and thyme

see opposite page 17

## serves 4

### Shopping List

2 tablespoons olive oil
1 onion, chopped
1 teaspoon thyme
2 tablespoons breadcrumbs
100 g/3½ oz dried
  apricots, diced
12 slices of topside of beef
½ egg, beaten
1 carrot, diced
1 celery stalk, diced
20 g/¾ oz butter
30 g/1¼ oz flour
1 teaspoon tomato purée
600 ml/1 pint beef stock
parsley, to garnish
salt and freshly ground
  black pepper

**1** To make the stuffing, heat half the olive oil in a large frying pan, and fry the onions until softened, but not brown.

**2** Add the thyme, crumbs and apricots and stir well. Cook for a further 2-3 minutes, and season to taste.

**3** Remove from the stove and mix in the beaten egg.

When I made this I used the crumbs
the starter (Muffins filled with leek and
smoked mackerel, page 18). This is good
served with cabbage and new potatoes.

4 Lay the beef slices on a flat
surface, and divide the stuffing
between them. Roll them up with
the ends folded in, to make a barrel
shape, and tie with string to keep
their shape.

5 Gently fry the beef parcels in
the remaining oil for 2-3
minutes to seal them. You may need
to do this in batches.

6 Transfer all the beef parcels to
a large casserole dish. Add
the carrot, celery and remaining
onion to the frying pan and fry
until the carrot is soft. Add the
butter and flour and cook for a
further 2 minutes.

7 Add the tomato purée and beef
stock. Bring to the boil, then
pour gently over the beef parcels.
Cover, and cook in a preheated
oven at gas mark 4/180°C/350°F
for 1 hour.

8 Once cooked, remove the
strings from the beef parcels
and season the sauce to taste. Strain
the sauce over the beef and serve
garnished with sprigs of parsley.

# Hungarian goulash with apple and celeriac rosti

## serves 4

### Shopping List

**FOR THE HUNGARIAN GOULASH**
50 g/2 oz lard
375 g/12 oz onions, sliced
1 kg/2 lb pork shoulder, cut into large chunks
500 g/1 lb tomatoes, peeled, quartered and deseeded
1 clove garlic, crushed
1 tablespoon paprika
1 bay leaf
1 teaspoon mixed herbs
1.2 litres/2 pints chicken stock

750 g/1½lb potatoes, peeled and cut into large cubes

**FOR THE APPLE AND CELERIAC ROSTI**
1 apple, cored, peeled and grated
2 potatoes, peeled and grated
½ celeriac, peeled and grated
4 tablespoons olive oil
salt and freshly ground black pepper

**1** Melt the lard in a large frying pan, then add the pork and onions and cook for 4-5 minutes until the pork starts to turn white.

**2** Add the tomatoes, garlic, paprika, bay leaf and mixed herbs and pour over the stock to cover. Bring to boil, turn down the heat, cover and simmer for 2 hours.

We Brits like to add sour cream to Hungarian Goulash, but that's not the way they do it in Hungary! However, if you like sour cream, stir in about 4 tablespoons at the end of the cooking time.

**3** Add the potatoes, stir well, and cook in a preheated oven at gas mark 5/ 375°F/190°C for 30-40 minutes until the potatoes are soft. Serve with the Apple and Celeriac Rosti.

## Apple and celeriac rosti

**1** Mix the apple, potatoes and celeriac, and season with salt and pepper.

**2** Heat the oil in a large frying pan, until bubbling, and place 4 medium-size, metal cutters in the pan. Place a quarter of the mixture in each cutter, pressing it down well with the back of a spoon. Remove the cutters, and cook for 10-15 minutes, turning once, until golden and crisp on the outside. Pat dry using kitchen paper.

# Couscous on the waves

| serves 4 |
| --- |

## Shopping List

- 2 x 500 g/1 lb packet couscous
- 3 tablespoons oil
- 4 courgettes, sliced
- 2 aubergines, cut into 1 cm/½ in cubes
- 2 cauliflowers, cut into florets and blanched
- 1 large red pepper, diced
- 1 large green pepper, diced
- 400 g/13 oz chick peas, drained
- 8 thick, spicy sausages, sliced
- 2 large onions, sliced
- 100 g/3½ oz roasted peanuts
- 1 tablespoon chopped mint
- 1 tablespoon chopped coriander leaves
- 750 g/1½ lb tinned, chopped tomatoes
- 3 cloves garlic, chopped
- 1 packet green chillies, split, deseeded and chopped

This was for a group of friends who were spending the day on a yacht. I didn't have much room to work, but it was good fun.

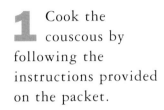

**1** Cook the couscous by following the instructions provided on the packet.

**2** Heat 2 tablespoons of the oil in a large frying pan, and gently fry the courgette, aubergine, cauliflower, peppers, chick peas, and sausage for 15 minutes. Separately fry the sliced onions in the remaining oil, until very crispy.

**3** Add the couscous to the vegetables, and then mix in the peanuts. Add the fried onions, mint and coriander, and heat through for 2-3 minutes.

**4** Meanwhile, make a very quick tomato sauce. Warm the chopped tomatoes in a large saucepan. Add the garlic and chillies and stir well. Cook for 5-6 minutes, until piping hot. Season to taste, and serve poured over the couscous.

# Glazed collar of bacon with Guinness

## serves 4

### Shopping List

1 kg/2 lb collar of bacon,
   soaked in cold water
   overnight
1 onion, chopped
1 leek, chopped
1 celery stick, chopped
12 cloves
1 small bunch parsley
2 bay leaves
2 sprigs thyme
1 small can Guinness
6 tablespoons black treacle
175 g/6 oz molasses sugar
100 ml/3½ fl oz apple juice
4 tablespoons honey
2 tablespoons mustard

We served this with Onion and Ginger Marmalade (page 65) and fried cabbage and roast potatoes.

**1** Put the soaked bacon in a large saucepan and surround with cold water. Bring to the boil.

**2** Add the onion, leek, celery, cloves, parsley, bay leaves and thyme. Reduce the heat and simmer for 1½ hours. Skim off any scum that appears. To test if the meat is done, put a knife in the bacon and lift up; if it is cooked, the joint will slide off easily.

**5** Meanwhile, mix the Guinness, black treacle, molasses sugar, apple juice, honey and mustard and smear over the bacon. Return to the oven and cook for a further 20-30 minutes.

**3** Remove the bacon, drain, and cut off the skin and fat. Score the surface of the joint into diamond shapes.

**4** Place the joint in a roasting dish and bake in a preheated oven at gas mark 7/425°F/220°C for 5 minutes.

**6** Leave the bacon to rest for 10 minutes before carving. This relaxes the meat and makes it tender.

# Sausage and bean pot with parsley dumplings

## serves 4

### Shopping List

- 1 tablespoon olive oil
- 8 chipolatas, cut in half
- 1 large onion, diced
- 6 slices middle bacon, diced
- 2 carrots, 1 cut into rings, 1 into ribbons
- 1 large courgette, sliced
- 1 red pepper, diced
- 6 tablespoons passata
- 400 g/13 oz tinned, whole tomatoes
- 300 ml/½ pint chicken or vegetable stock
- 1 vegetable stock cube
- 1 small tin cannellini beans
- 4 tablespoons self raising flour
- ½ packet vegetarian suet
- small handful parsley, chopped
- 1 sprig thyme, chopped
- 2-3 sage leaves, chopped

**1** Heat the oil in a large frying pan, and brown the chipolatas. Drain the sausages and reserve.

**2** Using the same pan, fry the onion until softened, but not brown. Add the bacon and cook for 2-3 minutes.

I made this for a whole nursery of young children (and their carers)! I think there were about 25 in total, but this version will serve 4 hungry children. It is designed to appeal to even the fussiest child, and to introduce them to new flavours and textures. It will also get some vegetables inside them!

**3** Stir in the carrot, courgettes, peppers, passata, tomatoes, stock and stock cube and cannellini beans, and season. Stir well.

**4** Cover, and cook over a medium heat for 45 minutes until the mixture is hot, with the vegetables and sausages cooked through.

**5** Meanwhile, make the dumplings. Sieve the flour into a large mixing bowl, and stir in the suet, chopped parsley, thyme and sage.

**6** Add sufficient water to mix to a soft but not wet dough. Shape into small dumplings. Add to the sausage mixture 10 minutes before the end of cooking time. They will be ready when the Sausage and Bean Pot is cooked.

# Pork chops with warm mushroom vinaigrette and stir-fried cabbage and apple

## serves 4

### Shopping List

2 tablespoons olive oil
4 pork chump chops
butter, for frying
1 white cabbage, sliced
2 Bramley apples, sliced
250 g/8 oz streaky
   bacon, diced
250 g/8 oz button
   mushrooms, sliced
2 cloves garlic, crushed
25 g/1 oz dried porcini
   mushrooms, reconstituted
   and chopped
3 tablespoons cider vinegar
3 tablespoons chopped parsley
salt and freshly ground
   black pepper

**1** Heat the oil in a large frying pan. Season the chops and fry for 1-2 minutes, on each side, until slightly browned. Bake in a preheated oven at gas mark 6/200°C/400°F for 12-15 minutes, depending on the thickness of the chops.

**2** Meanwhile, melt a knob of butter in a wok and stir-fry the cabbage and apple until soft, but not brown. Season with salt and pepper, remove from the pan, and keep in a warm place.

**3** To make the mushroom vinaigrette, first add the bacon to the pan and fry until golden brown and crispy.

**4** Stir in the button mushrooms and fry until they start to colour, and then add the garlic.

**5** Add the porcini mushrooms and cook for 2-3 minutes. Add any liquid that was used when reconstituting the porcini mushrooms, and boil quickly for 5 minutes to reduce the liquid.

**6** Stir in the vinegar and parsley and season well. Serve the chops placed on top of the stir-fried cabbage and apple and pour over the mushroom vinaigrette.

Plum baked Alaska
Cinnamon and hazelnut pavlova
Blueberry and orange clafoutis
Poached pears with chocolate sauce
Lemon tart
Tarte tatin
Raspberry and almond tart
Lemon surprise

Chocolate tart
White chocolate mousse
Triple chocolate terrine with raspberry coulis
Banoffee cheesecake with toffee pecan sauce
Flambéed bananas with rum
Plum and lemon pudding
Fruit flan
Fruit kebabs

# PUDD
# DESS

# INGS
# ERTS
&

# **P**lum baked Alaska

| serves 4 |
|----------|

## Shopping List

1 small tub vanilla ice cream
1 punnet of plums
25 g/1 oz butter
50 g/2 oz caster sugar
pinch of cinnamon
pinch of nutmeg
1 medium egg white

**1** Divide the ice cream between 4 heat- and freezer-proof serving bowls and place in a freezer.

**2** Cut the plums in half, and remove the stones.

**3** Melt the butter in a large frying pan, add the plums, half the sugar, cinnamon and nutmeg and cook for 2-3 minutes.

**4** Meanwhile, whisk the egg white with the remaining sugar until it forms stiff peaks.

**5** Remove the ice cream from the freezer and divide the plums between the bowls, placing them on top of the ice cream.

**6** Using an icing bag, pipe the meringue over the plums and place under a hot grill for about 5 minutes, until golden brown. Serve immediately.

# Cinnamon and hazelnut pavlova

| serves 4 |
| --- |

## Shopping List

3 medium egg whites
250 g/8 oz icing sugar
1 teaspoon cornflour
1 teaspoon vinegar
25 g/1 oz cinnamon
75 g/3 oz ground hazelnuts
300 ml/ ½ pint whipping
  cream
25 g/1 oz flaked almonds,
  lightly toasted

This is an easy way to make meringue a bit more interesting.

**1** Whisk the egg whites until they form stiff peaks, then fold in 175 g/6 oz of the icing sugar.

**2** Gently fold in the cornflour and vinegar, and then fold in the cinnamon and hazelnuts. Pile the meringue onto a baking sheet, lined with baking parchment, to form a rough circle.

**3** Bake in a preheated oven at gas mark ½/250°F/130°C for 1¼-1½ hours, and then leave to cool.

**4** Whisk the cream and remaining sugar together until stiff and then spoon over the meringue. Sprinkle with the flaked almonds, to serve.

# Blueberry and orange clafoutis

## Shopping List

125 g/4 oz flour
300 ml/ ½ pint milk
3 large eggs, beaten
75 g/3 oz icing sugar, plus
   a little for dusting
1 teaspoon vanilla essence
butter, for greasing
1 punnet of blueberries
1 orange (cut into segments,
   save the zest and any juice)

Clafoutis is a classic French dessert, and is a cross between a plump pancake and a pudding. It is very easy to prepare, and you can use any soft fruit. It is delicious served with crème fraîche or double cream.

**1** Gradually mix together the flour and the milk, and beat until smooth. Beat in the eggs, until smooth.

**2** Add the icing sugar and vanilla essence, and mix well.

**3** Lightly grease two small ovenproof dishes (about 10 cm/ 4 in diameter, 3 cm/1¼ in deep) and place the blueberries and orange segments with zest and juice in the bottom of the dishes.

**4** Pour the batter over the top of the fruit and bake in a preheated oven at gas mark 5/ 375°F/190°C for about 30 minutes, until the top of the clafoutis are light brown.

**5** Remove from the oven and, while still warm, sieve some icing sugar over the top, to serve.

" *I went to visit Helen and her two male flatmates in Ladbroke Grove on a chilly autumn day. Unlike many people in shared accommodation, they often eat together. Their favourites are roasts and stews, so I rang the changes with Fillet of Lamb en croûte (page 66), which is basically roast lamb – but with a twist! This clafoutis followed.* "

# Poached pears with chocolate sauce

| serves 4 |
| --- |

see opposite page 49

## Shopping List

125 ml/4 fl oz water
125 g/4 oz caster sugar
1 teaspoon vanilla essence
4 Comice pears
250 g/8 oz plain chocolate
150 ml/¼ pint single cream
1 packet flaked almonds,
   finely chopped

You could make this chocolate sauce in advance, if you prefer. It will be quite happy if you leave it for a couple of hours, and reheat when you are ready to dip the pears.

**1** Bring the water and the caster sugar to the boil. Reduce the heat, and simmer, stirring continuously, until the sugar is melted. Add the vanilla essence.

**2** Peel and core the pears, but try to keep the stalks attached. Place the pears in the pan, and simmer gently for 10 minutes.

**4** Meanwhile, break the chocolate into pieces and melt in a *bain-marie*, or in a bowl over a pan of simmering water. Warm the cream in another *bain-marie* or bowl over simmering water. Remove the chocolate and cream from the heat, stir until smooth and mix together.

**5** Remove the pears from the poaching liquid, drain, then, holding each pear at the top, coat the base with the chocolate mixture. Next, holding the pear by the stalk, coat the rest of it so that it is completely covered. Place in a fridge until the chocolate sets. Serve each pear sprinkled with the almonds.

*This was part of the menu for the Mitchell family (no, not that one...). They live in Barnes, and we could hear the planes while we were trying to film. They are a vegetarian family, so I made them a Green Bean Salad (page 15) to start, Leek and Mushroom Risotto (page 32) for a main course, and these Poached Pears. I suggested a healthy, fruit dessert, but there was a request for chocolate, so this combined the two.*

# Lemon tart

serves 6

## Shopping List

150 g/5 oz plain flour
75 g/3 oz butter, plus extra
   for greasing
200 g/7 oz caster sugar
5 lemons
2 eggs
2 egg yolks
150 ml/ ¼ pint single cream
150 ml/ ¼ pint double cream,
   whipped or crème fraîche

I made this to go with the
Salmon with Grain Mustard
Topping (page 42). It was
one of my favourite menus
of the series.

**1** To make the pastry, sieve the flour
into a bowl. Cut the butter into
pieces, add to the flour and rub with your
fingertips until it resembles fine
breadcrumbs. Stir in 25 g/1 oz of the caster
sugar, then add about a tablespoon of cold
water and mix to a firm dough.

**2** Knead the pastry on a lightly floured
surface. Roll out the pastry to make a
large circle and use to line a buttered,
medium-size, spring-form flan tin. Line
with foil, fill with baking beans, and
bake 'blind' in a preheated oven
at gas mark 6/400°F/200°C for
20 minutes.

**3** Remove from the oven, take out the beans and discard the foil, then reduce the oven temperature to gas mark 3/325°F/170°C.

**4** To make the filling, grate the rind from the lemons and squeeze the juice from two of these; reserve the unsqueezed lemons. Whisk the eggs, egg yolks and 125 g/4 oz sugar for about two minutes until frothy, then whisk in ¾ of the lemon rind, the lemon juice and single cream. Pour the filling into the pastry case, and bake for 30-40 minutes until the tart is set. Leave to cool.

**5** Place the remaining sugar in a pan with 150 ml/¼ pint water. Bring to the boil, stirring continuously until the sugar has dissolved. Add the remaining lemon rind and boil for 2-3 minutes until thickened. Drain, and reserve.

**6** When you are ready to serve the tart, spoon small scoops of the double cream or crème fraîche around the edge of the tart. Slice each of the reserved lemons, and place a lemon slice between each scoop and scatter over the grated lemon rind.

# Tarte tatin

| serves 4 |
| --- |

see opposite page 64

This is the French version of our beloved apple pie. I'm not entering into the debate about which came first; I'll just say they are both pretty good!

## Shopping List

flour, for dusting
250 g/8 oz puff pastry
125 g/4 oz butter
375 g/12 oz sugar
4 apples, peeled, cored
   and quartered
icing sugar, to dust
vanilla ice cream, to serve

**1** Roll out the pastry on a floured surface, to form a large circle. Use a large, deep frying pan as a template, and cut out the pastry to fit. Place the pastry to one side.

**2** Melt the butter in the pan and add the sugar. Stir until the butter starts to froth.

**3** Neatly arrange the apple quarters in the pan, peel side facing downwards, but do not stir.

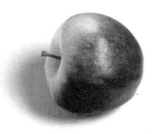

**4** Place the pastry on top of the pan, push down gently onto the apples, and tuck in the sides.

**5** Place the whole pan in an oven and bake at gas mark 5/375°F/190°C for 15 minutes.

**6** Remove from the oven, and carefully turn the tarte out onto a plate. You might need to reposition the apples a little. Dust with icing sugar and serve with vanilla ice cream.

*I was surrounded by lovely ladies when I made this – a perk of the job! We met at Dina's house and she invited her daughter, her mum, her mother-in-law, and her sister-in-law. They all live within about 10 minutes of each other, and all get on brilliantly. They take it in turns to cook for each other, and their favourite food is chips, so I made them Turkey Parcels with Potato Wedges and Roasted Tomatoes (pages 54-55), followed by this Tarte Tatin.*

# Raspberry and almond tart

serves 6-8

## Shopping List

1 packet shortcrust pastry
125 g/4 oz sugar
75 g/3 oz soft margarine, plus
   extra for greasing
1 large egg
1 large egg yolk
1 tablespoon brandy
50 g/2 oz blanched almonds
2 tablespoons plain flour
1 tablespoon double cream
1 punnet fresh raspberries

Blueberries would also work well with this tart.

**1** Grease a medium-size, round, spring-form flan tin. Roll out the pastry on a cold, lightly floured surface to make a large circle.

**2** Place the pastry over the tin and, using your thumbs, gently push the pastry down into the tin. Trim off the excess pastry.

**3** Cream the sugar and margarine together. Beat the egg and egg yolk together and gradually add to the margarine mixture.

**4** Add the brandy and stir in the almonds and flour.

**5** Add the double cream and stir. Pour the mixture into the flan dish and sprinkle the raspberries on top.

**6** Bake the tart on a hot baking sheet in a preheated oven at gas mark 7/ 425°F/220°C for 25 minutes.

# Lemon surprise

| serves 4 |
|:---:|

## Shopping List

75 g/3 oz butter, softened,
   plus extra for greasing
250 g/8 oz caster sugar
grated zest and juice of
   2 lemons
5 eggs, separated
50 g/2 oz self-raising flour
300 ml/½ pint milk
crème fraîche, to serve

This is a lovely, soft, lemon pudding, with a surprising middle.

**1** Beat the butter and sugar together until pale and fluffy. Beat in the lemon zest and juice.

**2** Beat in the egg yolks, one at a time, then add spoonfuls of flour alternately with the milk.

**3** Whisk the egg whites until stiff, and fold into the lemon mixture.

**4** Pour into a large, buttered soufflé dish and bake at gas mark 4/ 350°F/180°C for 40-45 minutes. Serve hot or cold with crème fraîche.

# **C**hocolate tart

## serves 6

### Shopping List

1 packet shortcrust pastry
250 g/8 oz plain chocolate
250g/8 oz unsalted butter,
   plus extra for greasing
125 g/4 oz dark Muscovado
   sugar
125 g/4 oz Demerara sugar
1 small packet cocoa powder
2 tablespoons instant coffee
6 tablespoons hot water
4 medium eggs

**1** Roll out the pastry to make a large circle, and use to line a buttered, medium-size, spring-form flan tin. Line with foil, fill with baking beans, and bake 'blind' in a preheated oven at gas mark 6/ 400°F/200°C for 20 minutes.

**2** Put the chocolate, butter and sugar in a *bain-marie* or in a bowl over a pan of simmering water, and stir until warm, smooth and melted.

**3** Mix the cocoa powder, coffee and the hot water, and stir until smooth.

**4** In a large mixing bowl, beat the eggs until frothy and then add all the other mixtures. Stir well.

**5** Pour into the pastry case and bake at gas mark 1/275°F/140°C for 40-45 minutes or until firm and risen. Serve warm or cold.

**Opposite** *Salmon in Filo Pastry with Dill Sauce (page 46), Banoffee Cheesecake with Toffee Pecan Sauce (100).*
**Overleaf** *Red Pepper and Basil Flan (page 28), Plum and Lemon Pudding (page 104).*

# White chocolate mousse

## serves 2

### Shopping List

175 g/6 oz white chocolate
75 ml/3 fl oz milk
2 medium egg whites
¼ teaspoon lemon juice
250 ml/8 fl oz double cream

You could use good-quality milk or dark chocolate instead of white for this recipe.

**1** Melt the chocolate in a *bain-marie*, or in a bowl over a pan of gently simmering water. When it has melted whisk in the milk until smooth, and leave to cool.

**2** In a separate bowl, whisk the egg whites with the lemon juice until they form stiff peaks, then gently fold into the chocolate mixture.

**3** Whisk the double cream until it forms soft peaks and fold into the chocolate mixture.

**4** Divide the mousse between two glasses or ramekin dishes, and cover with clingfilm. Chill for at least 2 hours.

# Triple chocolate terrine with raspberry coulis

## serves 4

see opposite page 48

### Shopping List

100 g/3½ oz dark chocolate
1 egg yolk, beaten
¼ cup strong coffee
300 ml/ ½ pint cream,
  lightly whipped
100 g/3½ oz milk chocolate
2 tablespoons rum
100 g/3½ oz white chocolate
½ sachet of gelatine
50 g/2 oz raspberries
1 teaspoon icing sugar

This looks very impressive, but is actually very simple. I served this cut into hearts, but slices look just as good.

**1** To make the dark chocolate mousse melt the dark chocolate in a *bain-marie*, or in a bowl over a pan of simmering water. Stir in the beaten egg yolk. Add the coffee and a third of the cream, and stir well.

**2** In a separate bowl, make the milk chocolate mousse by melting the chocolate in the same way as before. Mix in the rum and half of the remaining cream.

**3** Then make the white chocolate mousse. Melt the chocolate in the same way as before. Heat 2 tablespoons water, sprinkle the gelatine into the water and mix with a fork. If the gelatine doesn't all dissolve, heat very gently, until melted. Leave to cool a little before adding to the melted chocolate. Fold in the remaining cream.

**4** To assemble the terrine, line a terrine mould with clingfilm, pour in the milk chocolate mousse and mix, then set in the fridge. Repeat with the white chocolate mousse and then the dark chocolate mousse. Leave to chill for at least 6 hours, until set.

**5** Make the raspberry coulis by simmering the raspberries together with the icing sugar and a little water for five minutes. When the raspberries have broken down, push them through a nylon sieve and discard the pips. Allow to cool.

**6** To serve, slice the terrine into 4, and place each slice on a plate. Pour the raspberry coulis around each slice.

# Banoffee cheesecake with toffee pecan sauce

see opposite page 96

## Shopping List

- 100 g/3½ oz butter, melted
- 125 g/4 oz sweet oat biscuits, crushed
- 75 g/3 oz pecan nuts, chopped
- 6 medium bananas, sliced, and mixed with 3 tablespoons lemon juice
- 175 g/6 oz caster sugar
- 3 large eggs
- 375 g/12 oz curd cheese
- 200 g/7 oz fromage frais
- 75 g/3 oz soft brown sugar
- 50 g/2 oz granulated sugar
- 150 g/5 oz golden syrup
- 150 ml/¼ pint double cream
- 1 teaspoon vanilla essence

The oat biscuits used here add a lovely crunch that works well with the pecan nuts. Add a splash of rum to the sauce if you like.

**1** Melt 40 g/1½ oz of the butter in a large saucepan and add the biscuits and 40 g/1½ oz of the pecan nuts. Mix well, and spoon into the base of a medium-size, spring-form flan tin. Flatten using the back of a spoon, and bake in a preheated oven at gas mark 2/300°F/150°C for 15 minutes.

**2** To make the filling, blend half of the banana slices in a food processor until smooth, then add the caster sugar, eggs, curd cheese and fromage frais. Blend again, and pour over the biscuit base. Bake for 1 hour.

**3** Turn off the oven and leave the cheesecake inside to cool slowly until completely cold. This will prevent the cheesecake from cracking.

**4** To make the sauce, melt the remaining butter, brown and granulated sugars and the golden syrup over a low heat until smooth. Add the cream and stir until smooth. Add the remaining chopped pecan nuts and stir. Remove from the heat and allow to cool completely. Add a few drops of vanilla essence, and pour into a serving jug.

**5** Decorate the cheesecake with the remaining slices of banana and serve in thick slices, with the toffee pecan sauce poured around.

*" I had my work cut out cooking for Robin and Carol and their family, as Carol had done a Cordon Bleu cookery course, so she really knew her stuff! It was actually lots of fun, and Carol was a great help in the kitchen. She has a much lighter touch than me, and this was evident when we were handling the filo pastry for the Salmon in Filo Pastry with Dill Sauce (page 46). I learnt a thing or two! "*

# Flambéed bananas with rum

see opposite page 16

| serves 2 |
|---|

## Shopping List

25 g/1 oz butter
2 tablespoons brown sugar
zest of two oranges
4 tablespoons dark rum
2 bananas, peeled, and cut
　　into 3 pieces
clotted cream, to serve

I made this for a Jamaican family, using a wonderful rum they had brought back from a family visit.

**1** In a large frying pan, melt the butter and add the sugar, orange zest and half the rum.

**2** When the sugar has melted, add the bananas, and cook over a medium heat, for 3-4 minutes, until the bananas are golden and caramelised.

**3** Add the remaining rum and flambé using a match to light the alcohol.

**4** When the flames die out, serve with clotted cream.

*It was a joy cooking for June and Lionel Robinson and their two sons. I used to work near them, so it was a trip down Memory Lane for me. Not only did Lionel provide a wonderful Jamaican rum to go with this banana dish, he also cooked a meal for me to try! His speciality is Escabeche of Fish, and it is delicious. Maybe in another book...*

# Plum and lemon pudding

serves 4

see opposite page 97

## Shopping List

6 medium egg yolks
4 medium eggs
zest and juice of 4 lemons
325 g/11 oz caster sugar
175 g/6 oz unsalted butter,
  softened
6 tablespoons water
250 g/8 oz plums
sprig of mint, to decorate

This is very rich, and more-ish, so be warned. It is basically a luxurious, lemon-curd custard. You could vary the fruit according to the seasons.

**1** Place the egg yolks and whole eggs in a bowl. Add the lemon zest and juice and whisk together until frothy, then whisk in 25 g/1 oz sugar.

**2** Place the bowl over a pan of simmering water, and bring to the boil. Add half the butter and continue whisking until well mixed, and the mixture starts to thicken. Add the remaining butter and continue whisking over a gentle heat for about 3 minutes. Remove, and allow to cool, whisking from time to time.

**3** Cut the plums into quarters, and discard the stones. Bring the water and the remaining sugar to the boil. Stir until the sugar is melted, and add the plum quarters. Simmer gently for 3-4 minutes, until the plums are soft.

**4** Drain, then place the warm plums in a glass dish and cover with the warm egg mixture.

**5** Cool, then place in a fridge to set. Serve decorated with the sprig of mint.

> *Cooking for Bishop Coote and his grown-up children was fun. I heard all about the Bishop's travels abroad. He told me that working in Africa has made him appreciate how lucky we are to have such a wealth of food, and how it has made him frugal with food — leftovers never go to waste. Mrs Coote was away on business, and the Bishop promised to make my lunch of Red Pepper and Basil Flan (page 28) and this Plum and Lemon Pudding for her, when she returned.*

# Fruit flan

| serves 4 |
|---|

## Shopping List

75 g/3 oz caster sugar
3 medium eggs
75 g/3 oz plain flour
25 g/1 oz butter
1 small tin red cherries
2 tablespoons brandy, optional
2 tablespoons black cherry jam
300 ml/½ pint double cream,
  whipped

The sponge flan case in this recipe is fat-free, so very useful if you are trying to cut down on fat. Substitute crème fraîche for the double cream, if you like. You can vary the tinned fruit used, or use fresh fruit.

**1** Whisk together the sugar and eggs until thick and the mixture has doubled in size.

**2** Fold in the flour and pour into a well-greased, 20 cm/8 in spring-form flan tin. Bake at gas mark 7/425°F/220°C for 8-10 minutes. Remove, and leave to cool.

**3** Melt the butter and add the cherries and brandy. Cook for 2-3 minutes.

**4** Spoon the cherry mixture into the flan case, and pour any leftover juices into the black cherry jam.

**5** Gently warm the black cherry jam, then spoon over the cherries.

**6** Decorate the edge of the flan with the whipped double cream.

*"Cooking for the Liddell family was certainly different... I cooked in a caravan for the first time! The Liddells love caravanning, and have gone away almost every weekend for the past 8 years. Their caravan was well-equipped, and even had a full-size gas cooker, so I cooked Pork Chops with Warm Mushroom Vinaigrette and Stir-fried Cabbage and Apple (page 80), with this Fruit Flan for pudding."*

# **F**ruit kebabs

serves 4

## Shopping List

2 red apples, peeled,
   cored and cut into
   wedges
1 large banana, peeled
   and cut into 8 pieces
2 nectarines, peeled and
   cut into wedges
2 kiwi fruit. peeled and
   cut into wedges
½ medium pineapple,
   peeled and cut into
   wedges

2 mangoes, peeled and cut
   into wedges
juice of 1 lemon
4 tablespoons honey
50 g/2 oz butter
oil or butter, for frying
icing sugar, to serve
sprigs of mint, to serve

I made these to follow the Sausage and Bean Pot (page 78). Needless to say, as they were for children, I removed the skewers before serving. If using wooden skewers, soak in water before using.

**1** Feed the fruit alternately onto 4 kebab skewers. Arrange however you like, but try to balance the different colours.

**2** Squeeze the lemon juice over the kebabs to prevent the fruit from going brown.

**3** Melt the butter and add the honey, and stir until the butter starts to froth.

**4** Drizzle a barbecue or griddle pan with the oil or butter for frying. When very hot, add your kebabs. Rotate as they start to colour, spooning over the honey and butter glaze from time to time.

**5** When the kebabs look nicely golden and caramelised, serve with any remaining glaze. Sprinkle with icing sugar and garnish with mint sprigs, to serve.

# **Index**

Index
111

## Index
## 112